Copyright

All rights reserved. Without above, no part of this publication may be produced, stored in or introduced into a retrieval system or transmitted in any form or by any means (electronic, mechanical, photocopying or otherwise) without the prior written permission of the copyright owner and publisher of this Travel Guide.

We have relied on our own experience as well as many different sources for this Travel Guide, and we have done our best to check facts and to give credit where it is due. In the event that any material is incorrect or has been used without proper permission, please contact us so that the oversight can be corrected.

Cover photo by David Kostner / Wikimedia

Written by: Angela Pearse

Edited by: Bruno Luis

Contents

Introduction to Munich	3
#1 Marienplatz	4
#2 Oktoberfest	6
#3 English Garden	8
#4 Deutsches Museum	10
#5 BMW Museum	12
#6 Nymphenburg Palace	14
#7 Munich Residenz	16
#8 BMW Welt	18
#9 Allianz Arena	20
#10 Alte Pinakothek	22
#11 Hofbrauhaus Munchen	24
#12 St. Peter's Church	26
#13 Olympiapark	28
#14 Viktualienmarkt	30
#15 Asam's Church	32
#16 Frauenkirche	34
#17 New Town Hall	36
#18 Hellabrunn Zoo	38
#19 Neue Pinakothek	40
#20 Theatine Church	42
Map of Attractions in Central Munich	44
Map of Attractions in Outer Munich	45

Introduction to Munich

Bavaria's lively capital is known for its outstanding architecture, world class museums and famous Oktoberfest beer festival. Amazingly, Munich's stunning historic centre looks exactly like it did in the 1800s, though allied bomb attacks in World War II destroyed much of it.

Thanks to an intensive and dedicated rebuilding period after the war, which kept to original plans, today beautiful buildings like the Altes Rathaus, Frauenkirche and Alte Pinakothek can still be admired and visited today in the spirit of their creation.

But Munich isn't just a city stuck in the past. Home to many multinational companies and at the forefront of technology and science, it's one of Germany's most prosperous and forward thinking cities.

This fascinating mix of traditional values and business nous is why it has earned the nickname 'the city of laptops and lederhosen'. From beer halls to BMW, join us as we visit some of the best things to see and do in the city of Munich!

#1 Marienplatz

© Wikimedia / Chris 73

Any journey to Munich will undoubtedly start with a visit to Marienplatz. This is the city's picturesque central square which dates back to the 12th century. It is a popular tourist spot for its beautiful architecture (notably the New Town Hall, the Mariensäule and the Old Town Hall), shops, restaurants and people watching.

A favourite attraction is the Glockenspiel in the New Town Hall which draws the crowds, especially when the dancing figures come out to perform for a 15 minute long show. The clock is set to entertain at 11am, 12pm and 5pm, so it is best to get there early so you have a good view. Note that the 5pm show doesn't occur during winter.

Marienplatz was named after the column in the centre of the square called the Mariensäule (Marian Column) which is a religious column featuring a gold statue of the Virgin Mary on top. This was originally in the Frauenkirche, Munich's landmark Roman Catholic Church, situated around a five minute walk from the square. The Mariensäule column was erected in 1638 to celebrate the Swedish finally leaving the city during the Thirty Years War and as a dedication to Mary to protect the town from cholera.

At this time the square was used as a market place and for tournaments and executions, but in 1807 the market was moved as the city grew in size. The much larger Viktualienmarkt to the southeast is where you will find around 140 stalls offering all manner of fresh fare.

The grandest building in Marienplatz is the New Town Hall, or simply Rathaus. The monumental building is Flemish Gothic in style and with its 85 metre tower it dominates the north east side of the square. Again, like the Viktualienmarkt, it was built as a solution to the Old Town Hall simply being too small to accommodate the city's administration offices.

The beautiful architecture can be admired, as well as the Glockenspiel show, and you can also go up in the lift inside the tower for magical views of the city.

© Flickr / digital cat

Marian Column

Other highlights of the Marienplatz include the Old Town Hall, a Gothic style building destroyed by bombers in World War II and completely rebuilt to its original 15th century plans.

The Fish Fountain is a relaxing place to have a break and munch on pastry while you're waiting for the Glockenspiel to start, and between Karlsplatz and Marienplatz you'll find numerous restaurants and shops. This can get crowded in the weekends, so try and go midweek if your schedule allows.

#2 Oktoberfest

© Wikimedia / Usien

Munich swells in size from late September to early October as visitors flock to the world's biggest beer festival, Oktoberfest. Held over 16 days, the festival is not only about drinking as much of the local brew as possible, it is also a fun fair with many attractions such as rides, stalls, games and food.

The extensive fairgrounds where Oktoberfest is situated are called Theresienwiese, locals shorten this to Wiesn. The annual festival has been going since 1810 with just 24 occasions when it did not take place, including during World War II from 1939 to 1945.

Though no one is entirely sure of its origins, it is said to have been an after party to celebrate the royal wedding of Prince Ludwig to Princess Therese in 1810. After five days of festivities, one of the sergeants in the National Guard proposed horse races and a beer festival be held in their honour.

From that time on Oktoberfest became an unofficial annual event which grew in size every year it was held. As well as horse races, there was tree climbing, swings, bowling and more. In 1818, a carnival was introduced to accompany the beer tents.

A committee was formed in 1819 to take charge of the organisation and from then on it became an official annual event. For a couple of years after World War II whilst Germany recovered, Oktoberfest was called 'Autumn Fest' and there was just normal beer rather than the proper Oktoberfest beer which is quite strong.

Other compromises during its history include the 'quiet Oktoberfest' which was introduced in 2005 to make it a suitable festival for families and older people. This concept has curbed things getting out of control during the day with pop music only played after 6pm.

With around 7 million litres of beer consumed at this festival in previous years, as you can imagine it can get a little rowdy. The festival starts off at 12pm with traditional parades involving the barmaids and barmen which end up at the Wiesn grounds. There is no entrance fee as such for the tents which have both indoor and outdoor seating. There are around 14 big tents and a number of smaller ones. The larger tents can seat up to 5,000 people!

© Flickr / leigh wolf

Oktoberfest

You can reserve seats but if you don't it pays to get there early as the popular tents, such as the Hofbrau tent which attracts international visitors, fill up quickly.

Dressing up in a traditional German costume (dirndl for women, lederhosen for men) isn't mandatory but you'll feel out of place if you don't. Be sure to try the local fare (delicious and plentiful) and the carnival which is great fun.

#3 English Garden

© Flickr / Heribert Pohl

The English Garden, or 'Englischer Garten' in German, is an extensive urban green space that runs from the centre of Munich to the north of the city. At 3.7 square km it is the largest public park in Europe. Apart from being an extremely pleasant place to stroll in any season, there are a number of interesting attractions including two beer gardens, a river to surf on, a Japanese tea house, a Greek temple, numerous bird species and over 100 bridges.

The English Garden gets its name from the type of gardens popular in England during the mid-18th century to the early 19th century. These were more relaxed than the formal French and Italian style with meandering paths, architectural features and ponds. The park in Munich was originally created by Archduke Carl Theodor as a military park for soldiers to relax in, but it was renamed the English Garden in the late 1700s.

The English Garden has two sections, the Hirschau or northern section which is generally more peaceful, and the southern section which is nearer the city and busier. Each section has its own beer garden, which in summer months prove popular with locals and tourists alike.

Other popular activities in summer include cycling the park's many paths, picnicking, watching the skilled surfers ride the artificial waves of the Eisbach River, nude sunbathing (permitted since the 1960s) and self-guided walking tours.

The highlights of the English Garden in terms of monuments and features are as follows. In the southern section is the Hofgarten, a small formal park with a temple and war memorial, and a good place to start a walking tour. Near here is Prince Karl's Palace, an early 19th century mansion and the House of Art which has interesting temporary exhibitions.

The Greek-style temple Monopteros makes for excellent photo opportunities, while the Chinese Tower Beer Garden is a lively place where you can grab a beer and bratwurst, and mingle with the locals whilst listening to traditional music.

© Flickr / digital cat

The Monopteros

There is another beer garden located near the Kleinhesseloher Lake in the northern section of the garden, as well as the Seehaus Restaurant which overlooks the lake for which you can rent paddle boats.

You won't find as many tourists in this upper section of the garden, so the restaurants and food are more authentic. It's also worth making a detour to the Tivoli Kraftwerk Museum situated on the river if you have time.

#4 Deutsches Museum

The Deutsches Museum is one of most popular attractions in Munich and the largest museum of science and technology in the world. It has an estimated 1.5 million visitors a year and exhibits around 28,000 objects. For anyone interested in technology and its history this is a must-visit, be sure to set aside at least three to four hours, there is a lot to see.

The museum is scenically situated on an island in the Isar River in the centre of town. Its foundations sit on over 1,500 piles which go seven metres deep into the island. Originally called Coal Island, this was the site of the museum chosen back in 1903 when its instigator, Oskar von Miller an electrical engineer, became passionate about creating a science and technology museum. The actual building of the museum, which took ten years, was financed by Prince Ludwig.

The Deutsches Museum finally opened on 2 May 1925, Oskar von Miller's 70th birthday. The first exhibit displayed was an 18th century mercury thermometer with a Réaumur scale. Be sure to check out the permanent exhibition on the first floor with photographs, audio documents and films providing clarity on the history of this important museum.

During World War II, the museum operated on a tight budget under Nazi control. Many exhibits became outdated and then bombings in 1944 destroyed many exhibits and much of the building itself. Nevertheless it reopened after four years of reconstruction in 1948.

Notable architectural features of the reinforced concrete building include its Meteorological Tower which measures weather conditions. Inside the tower there is a Foucault pendulum which demonstrates the rotation of the earth.

The main part of museum has an incredible array of objects dedicated to 50 science and technology fields, and arranged over eight floors. There are too many to list here but highlights include the work bench where the atom was first split, lightning demonstrations, the first car ever made, the development of computers and astronautics, and a new technology section with robots. There are many interactive exhibits which will keep children and adults alike fascinated.

© Wikimedia / Andreas Fränzel

A Steam Engine in the Deutsches Museum

Kids Kingdom is especially great for children between the ages of three and eight and has a number of fun interactive activities. The inner courtyard also has several outdoor exhibits including massive water turbines, a weather station and, for those that need a break, a cafe and a shop.

#5 BMW Museum

© Wikimedia / Guido Radig

Car manufacturer BMW is one of the largest companies in Munich, but it is also one of the most popular tourist attractions for its auto museum. The museum is situated next to the BMW tower and affectionately known as the 'salad bowl'. You will need to allocate at least two hours, perhaps even more if you're crazy about cars.

As a company BMW has been around since 1913 and originally focused on building airplane engines. They shifted to motorbikes in 1923 and then automobiles in 1928.

World War II severely disrupted production due to Allied Forces dismantling BMW factories but the company survived on producing bicycles and household appliances.

From 1950 BMW was back in force and decided to solely produce luxury cars, a move that has seen them become one of the most respected car makers in the world today. The museum therefore was constructed as a dedication to the technical development of BMW throughout its history.

The museum's modern design was called 'futuristic' when it was created in the 1970s. It was the work of Viennese architect Karl Schwanzer, who also designed the BMW Headquarters, the 100 metre 4 cylinder tower alongside.

The museum has both permanent and temporary exhibitions featuring a plethora of engines, motorbikes, cars and other vehicles which claim the BMW stamp.

A visit starts at the bottom of a spiral ramp which winds upwards to seven different themed houses with exhibits showcasing design inspiration, the company history, the development of the motorcycle, engines, motor sport, BMW advertising and development of the BMW series. In total there are over 100 BMW cars from the 1920s, to current models.

© Wikimedia / Wing1990hk

BMW Museum Interior

As well as cars, there are many slide shows and interactive exhibits and even a small cinema to provide further information on technology. Further exhibitions include the BMW Roadster and futuristic visions of clean energy cars to come.

Information is given in English and German and visitors can also purchase an audio guide for a small fee. Guided tours are available for either 1 ½ hours or 3 hours depending on your budget and schedule.

#6 Nymphenburg Palace

© Flickr / ho visto nina volare

Nymphenburg Palace is the Baroque residence of the rulers of the House of Wittelsbach. The palace and accompanying gardens are one of the top tourist attractions in Munich with hundreds of thousands of people visiting annually. Situated just west of Munich, the best way to reach the palace is by one of the city trams from the city centre. For those who wish to get a glimpse of the aristocratic life of a bygone era, you're in for a real treat.

The palace was commissioned in 1664 by Ferdinand Maria, the Electoral Prince of Bavaria, as a family summer retreat (the title of 'electoral prince' means that he was able to vote in the election of the Holy Roman Emperor). Designed by architect Agostino Barelli, it initially consisted of the central pavilion which he designed to resemble an Italian villa. The palace was expanded considerably during the 18th century by Ferdinand's son, Maximilian

Emanuel, and then by four other rulers.

Galleries, pavilions, room extensions, an orangery and stables were all architectural additions. Further interior refurbishment includes the Grand Hall by François Cuvilliés, a Flemish architect famous for his Rococo decorations. Each palace room is individually styled with its own colour scheme, wallpapers and paintings. Some of the rooms retain their original Baroque styling, while others bear the decorations of the rococo or neoclassical period.

With their vibrant ceiling paintings and massive chandeliers, all the rooms provide a practical function as well as an opulent setting for royalty. The central part of the palace is sectioned into north and south apartments with bedrooms and antechambers, while in the corridors connecting the outer wings you'll find the Coat of Arms Room and Max Emanuel's Great Gallery of Beauties (five portraits of ladies from the court of Louis XIV).

The south wing is called the Queen's Apartment after Queen Caroline who married Max I Joseph in 1797 and features an audience chamber, bedroom and study. One of highlights of visiting the palace is the Marstallmuseum, which is housed in the stables and features a collection of archaic carriages used over the centuries. There is also the wonderful collection of Nymphenburg porcelain.

© Wikimedia / Florian Adler

Gardens of Nymphenburg Palace

As well as the palace there are the extensive palace gardens to explore. Classically French they cover 200 hectares and are dotted with lakes, fountains, sculptures and pavilions. These were designed by Charles Carbonet, an employee of André Le Nôtre who designed the Versailles Palace gardens.

#7 Munich Residenz

© Wikimedia / Patrick Theiner

Moving from the summer residence to the royal palace, the Munich Residenz is the stunning city home of the former Bavarian monarchs from 1385 to 1918. Located in the heart of Munich, this is Germany's largest city palace. With over 120 rooms chock full of treasures you'll need several hours to view all that's on offer at this massive complex.

One of the most fascinating things about the Munich Residenz, apart from its size, is the conglomeration of different architectural styles that have been melded together over four centuries to form the palace complex. There are three main buildings to the complex, the Königsbau, the Alte Residenz and the Festsaalbau.

The Königsbau, or King's Building, dates back to the time of King Ludwig I of Bavaria and is essentially a palace extension modelled on the Palazzo Pitti in Florence. Built between 1825 and 1835 by the king's architect Leo von Klenze, the building is 30 metres high and contains royal living rooms and state apartments. Some of these were destroyed during World War II but what exists has been preserved.

The Alte Residenz, or Old Residenz, as the name suggests is the oldest part of the palace. Dating from 1385, the palace grew from an initial building called the Neuveste 'new fortress' constructed by the Wittelsbach dukes. The Gothic foundations and vaults belonging to this original castle can still be viewed.

Under four successive rulers the Neuveste was expanded to include banqueting halls, extra rooms, ballrooms, chapels, galleries, apartments and courtyards. Finally in the 19th century the major expansion work on this building was completed. The Alte Residenz is a good example of the variety of architectural additions over the centuries, with Renaissance, Baroque, Rococo and Neo-Classicism all making an appearance.

The Festsaalbau was built by King Ludwig I and is a neo-classical structure that is 250 metres long. It contained the king's throne room and reception halls, now home to a concert hall and theatre. His successor King Ludwig II commissioned a Winter Garden which included an ornamental lake, a grotto, and artificial rainbows and moonlight. Eventually this was dismantled as the lake started leaking through to the rooms below. Its memory lives on in sketches.

© Wikimedia / MagentaGreen

The Exterior of the Munich Residenz

Must-see highlights of the Munich Residenz include the magnificent Renaissance banqueting hall, the 'Antiquarium' with its 16th and 17th century frescoes, the Treasury which houses the Wittelsbach dynasty jewels, and the Ancestral Gallery with the family portraits hung in an ornate Baroque hall. Venture outside and you'll discover 10 courtyards, each with their own unique fountains and statues, and the 17th century French style palace garden created by King Maximilian I.

#8 BMW Welt

© Flickr / Oliver Kratzke

Adjacent to the BMW Headquarters and BMW Museum is the BMW Welt, or 'BMW World'. This multi-functional facility is the final piece in the triangle of BMW buildings offering a venue to showcase new BMW models, BMW themed shops and the latest auto innovations.

It's also a conference centre with an auditorium that holds 800 people, and there are gourmet restaurants, a bar, and cafes.

Even if you're not a car lover, the BMW Welt is still worth a look for its costly architecture and to view this remarkable work of art. Built between 2003 and 2007, the cost of the modern venue eventually came in at US$200 million.

The opening was supposed to coincide with the 2006 FIFA

World Cup but it ran over schedule and opened the following year. Known for their visionary projects, Austrian architects Coop Himmelblau have designed a futuristic masterpiece which has been likened to a 'triangular cloud of steel'.

BMW Welt has a solar powered roof 45 metres in diameter with 16,500 square metres of solar panels and it weighs 720 tonnes. This sits atop a double twisted cone covered in 10mm thick tempered glass.

The interior spaces are covered in UV protected stainless steel panels and have balconies suspended in air, curving bridges and monumental stairways.

Visitors to the BMW Welt are invited to take a look behind the scenes and discover, not just the fascinating architecture, but the latest cars and technology innovations taking place at BMW.

A wide range of BMW cars and motorbikes are showcased and you can even sit behind the wheel of your desired model and perhaps even go for a drive.

© Flickr / Matthias Ott

BMW Welt Interior

If you can't afford a BMW you can console yourself with a souvenir model at the gift shop and a drink at the bar.

For those keen to learn more about the BMW Welt there are two short tours held in English which you can join on the day, BMW Welt Tour Compact and the BMW Welt Architecture Tour for €7 per person, each is 1 hour 20 minutes in length. The longer Premium Tour covers the BMW Museum, the BMW Plant and BMW Welt runs for 3 hours and costs €22 per person.

#9 Allianz Arena

© Wikimedia / Richard Bartz

Another futuristic-looking venue is Munich's football stadium Allianz Arena. Located in the north of the city this is the home ground for professional football clubs FC Bayern Munich and TSV 1860 Munich.

As a visitor attraction, the Allianz Arena has much to offer football lovers and non-lovers alike with guided tours, a museum and visitor shop, and makes for an interesting half-day excursion.

In 2002 a public poll was held to decide if the stadium should be built, two thirds of people voted in its favour. Swiss architects Herzog & de Meuron came up with the eye-catching design which took three and half years to complete. Due to its exterior of inflated ETFE plastic panels, the arena is affectionately known as 'the inflatable boat'.

The innovative panels are made from a fluorine based plastic called Ethylene tetrafluoroethylene (EFTE). EFTE panels have been used in many modern architectural projects around the world and are known for being durable and heat resistant.

These properties are why the Allianz Arena boasts the world's first color-changing exterior featuring white, red, or blue colours at night, depending on the team playing.

The arena's seating capacity is legally 69,000 spectators but this has increased to 75,000 with lower tiered seating being converted to standing room to fit in extra people.

The innovative roof has roller blinds that can be opened or closed to block out sunlight interference and to shelter spectators when it's raining.

There are 190 TV screens around the 105 metre x 68 metre ground so you don't miss a minute of the game and lastly, it has Europe's largest underground car park.

You can experience the Allianz Arena by purchasing tickets to a football game or by taking one of the guided tours of the stadium which run daily throughout the year apart from Christmas, New Year's Eve, New Year's Day and home match days.

© Flickr / JasonParis

A Football Match taking Place at the Allianz Arena

The comprehensive tours cover the stadium, player's tunnel, dressing rooms, press room and FC Bayern Erlebniswelt, the football club's onsite museum.

#10 Alte Pinakothek

© Flickr / David Holt

The art museum Alte Pinakothek is the classic branch of Munich's arts district 'Kunstareal' of which there are two other galleries, the Neue Pinakothek and the Pinakothek der Moderne.

The Alte Pinakothek, or Old Pinakothek, is famous for being one of the world's oldest art museums and for its extensive collections of Old Master Paintings. If you're a classic art enthusiast, then you shouldn't miss this museum.

The Alte Pinakothek dates back to the time of King Ludwig I who in 1826 commissioned his architect Leo von Klenze to build a new gallery for the Wittelsbach collection. At the time the red brick museum was the largest in the world and had a number of modern features, such as skylights.

Neo-classical in design, it didn't try to be anything other than a museum, moving away from the typical castle-like structure of other galleries.

Therefore when it was opened in 1836 it led the way for other museums in Germany and Europe. Unfortunately bombing during World War II severely damaged the museum but it was reconstructed and was open again for public viewing in the 1950s.

Many people visit the Alte Pinakothek for the enormous 17th century painting 'Last Judgment' by Flemish Baroque painter Rubens which is six metres high and one of the largest canvasses by an Old Master. Suffice to say there are many Rubens paintings to be found here as the museum has the world's largest collection.

But this is just one of the reasons for visiting, the Alte Pinakothek displays over 800 paintings from the Netherlands, Italy, France, Spain and Germany covering the period from the 14th to the 18th century.

Important artists include Italian Renaissance painters Raphael, Giotto, da Vinci, Tintoretto and Botticelli. While Dutch and German painters such as Holbein, Rembrandt and Bosch are also represented, as well as Spanish artists, like Diego Velasquez.

© Flickr / David Holt

Inside the Alte Pinakothek

Visitors wanting to learn more about the artwork exhibited can go on a guided tour or rent an audio guide. Special exhibitions are held throughout the year focusing on different themes of European painting from the Middle Ages to the 18th century.

#11 Hofbrauhaus Munchen

HofBrauhaus is the most famous beer hall in the world. Dating back to the 16th century it's legendary for its rowdy vibe, traditional food and entertainment and vast quantities of beer consumed.

HofBrauhaus is just a five minute walk from Marienplatz in Platzl square and is an iconic tourist attraction. This is the best place to go if you want to be surrounded by jovial locals dressed in lederhosen.

The HofBrauhaus brewery was founded in 1589 by Duke Wilhelm V whose royal household wanted a beer more to their tastes. Initially a dark brown beer was produced near where the beer hall is situated today. In the early 1600s the duke's son, Maximilian I switched the brewery's sole focus to wheat beer, which was what he preferred.

Due to the brewery having the monopoly on this wheat beer it became very popular and, with the addition of new brews, the industry moved several times to accommodate production. Now owned by the Bavarian state government, the HofBrauhaus brewery produces many different beers, including wheat beer, Helles, Maibock and Dunkel and the famous Oktoberfest beer.

A traditional Bavarian style beer hall, the HofBrauhaus was built in the late 19th century and designed by architect Max Littmann. Its purpose was to provide a restaurant and entertainment venue for beer-loving patrons.

During World War II most of the beer hall was severely damaged but it has been rebuilt to its original plans. Hundreds of intact traditional beer mugs 'steins' were rescued from the basement. Some interesting architectural details include cross-vaulting, tables dating to 1897, bay windows, arched windows and vaulted ceilings painted with frescoes.

There are three floors to the HofBrauhaus and the ground floor 'Schwemme' is where most tourists end up. With long rows of tables seating up to 1,300 people, locals chatting to all and sundry, and waitresses hefting up to 10 steins at once it is a lively experience. You can munch on specialities such as roasted pork knuckle, wiener schnitzel and ox goulash while listening to German oom-pah music.

© Wikimedia / Jorge Royan

The Beer Hall

Upstairs in the Braustuberl you can expect a slightly quieter atmosphere, with a number of individual tables and seating for 145 people.

The top floor Festival Hall seats 900 and has a large entertainment stage for evening programmes of traditional Bavarian dance and music. An outdoor beer garden set under chestnut trees is a pleasant place in summer, it seats 400.

#12 St. Peter's Church

© Wikimedia / Andrew Bossi

The oldest parish church in the heart of Munich, St Peter's Church (Peterskirche) is popular with locals and tourists alike. Just a short stroll from Marienplatz, the Gothic-Romanesque church is visited for its beautiful Baroque interiors, gem-studded relic St. Mundita and the spectacular views afforded by the bell tower.

Locals have affectionately dubbed the church Alter Peter 'Old Peter' as there has been a church on this site since medieval times, even before Munich was officially founded as a city in 1158. The church then was wooden and built by monks.

The original burnt down and was replaced in the 14th century by a Romanesque church with Gothic motifs. A Renaissance tower appeared in the 17th century and then a Baroque choir in the 18th century. A Rococo renovation completed the church's architectural ensemble.

However, the current version is a reconstruction of the original which was badly damaged in World War II, this was only completed in the year 2000.

Art masterpieces in the church's ornate Baroque interior to look out for include the ceiling fresco by 18th century German painter and stucco plasterer Johann Baptist Zimmermann (restored in 1999 – 2000), a 15th century sculpture of St Peter by Erasmus Grasser, Gothic paintings by Jan Polack and altars by Ignaz Gunther.

The most gruesome, but equally fascinating, sight is that of St. Mundita, a Christian martyr who died around 300 AD. Her skeletal remains were transported from the catacombs in Rome to Munich in 1675. You can find the bejewelled relic in one of the side altars in a glass shrine.

Be sure to make time to climb the some 300 steps of the tower for excellent views of the city which on a clear day stretch all the way to the Alps. If you start your climb of the tower at 10.30am you can time it just right for the clock show on the town hall in Marienplatz at 11.00am.

© Wikimedia / H. Helmlechner

Interior of the Church

There is a small charge to access the viewing platform which is 56 metres high. The lower platform has colour-coded circles which inform visitors of the quality of the view from the top; white is for the best visibility.

#13 Olympiapark

© Flickr / Ole.Pophal

Olympiapark was constructed for the Summer Olympics in 1972 but still continues to be used as a recreational centre and event venue, and is a popular tourist attraction. Located in Oberwiesenfeld, there are four sections to the park: the Olympic Area, Olympic Village, Olympic Media City and Olympic Park.

The planners of Olympiapark for the 20th Olympic Games always meant for it to serve Munich afterwards as a venue for sporting, cultural and social events. The overall concept was a future forward design.

The vacant airfield of Oberwiesenfeld was chosen and a team of landscape architects and engineers, Gunther Behmisch, Frei Otto & Partners, set about producing the Olympic site which today covers 850,000 square metres.

Costing 1.35 billion Deutsch Marks and taking four years to build, the park's stadium, hall and swimming pool are covered by a high-tech tensile roof which makes the facilities usable in all seasons.

The park has many recreational facilities on offer to the public including an ice-rink, swimming pool, lake walks, cycle paths, picnic spots and a football stadium.

High profile winter sports such as: skiing, snowboarding, ice hockey and ice skating are held here and attract international competitors.

The landscape of Olympiapark is quite hilly since it is made up from the city's rubble from World War II transported here after the war. Its 60 metre Olympiaberg is perfect for slalom skiing in winter and in summer visitors can climb the mountain for great views of Olympiapark and the city.

You'll also find Munich's highest beer garden, Olympia Alm, up here and open in all weathers. For further views The Olympiaturm, a 290 metre TV tower, has a lift and a revolving restaurant at the top. The Olympic Stadium also offers a roof climb for anyone wanting a birds-eye-view of the grounds.

© Flickr / emdees

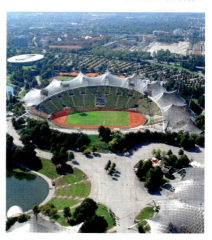

The Olympiastadion

Events and festivals taking place at Olympiapark during the year include the Tollwood Summer Festival with concerts and theatre productions, and free open air concerts at the Theatron (an amphitheatre on the lake). The Sea-Life Centre is also popular with families.

#14 Viktualienmarkt

© Wikimedia / Helmlechner

For a true taste of Munich, be sure to visit the Viktualienmarkt near Marienplatz. This daily food market is great for food lovers who want to try local dishes or pick up some fresh ingredients for a picnic. With 140 stalls and shops offering baked goods, local dishes, fresh produce, meats, fish and cheeses, there is something here to suit everyone.

The best time to visit the Viktualienmarkt is at lunchtime when it is buzzing with locals and tourists alike and there are plenty of choices for a quick bite. Saturday morning is also a pleasant time to walk around and grab a coffee or beer and check out the fresh fare and crafts.

The Viktualienmarkt started out as a small market in Marienplatz where farmers sold their grain and other food products necessary for daily life. As Munich grew, King Maximilian I declared in 1807 that the market would be moved to a larger space close by.

Several buildings were demolished to make way for it and this new market was called 'Marktplatz and later named Viktualienmarkt, 'viktualien' being the Latin word for food.

Expansion was again required in 1823 and more halls and pavilions were added over the years when required. The market had separate sections for fish, meat, flowers and the bakery.

During World War II, like many other parts of central Munich, the Viktualienmarkt was severely damaged. Afterwards it was almost demolished but due to its long history and importance the city decided to renovate it, adding fountains, statues and restaurants, turning it a focal point for locals to meet.

Fully pedestrianized since 1975, the market now covers around five and half acres and hosts several traditional annual events such as a gardener's day, brewer's day, summer festival and Shrove Tuesday dance. As well as having lots of stalls with different foods and crafts to check out, there are restaurants and beer gardens with plenty of outdoor seating.

© Flickr / La Citta Vita

The Beer Garden

Official opening hours for the Viktualienmarkt are from Monday to Saturday 8am to 8pm but some stalls and shop operate outside of standard times, like flower shops, bakeries and restaurants which have special opening hours.

The Viktualienmarkt is also well-situated for many central city attractions and public transportation.

#15 Asam's Church

Diego Delso, Wikimedia Commons, License CC-BY-SA 3.0

This small gem of a church is tucked away in the shopping street of Sendlinger Strasse. Asam's Church is a highly rated attraction in Munich though people usually stumble across it unwittingly.

The church is unusual for the fact that it was privately built by two brothers: Egid Asam and Cosmas Asam, and that it is breathtakingly ornate. The brothers, who were architects, lived beside the church in a 16th century house that they also renovated.

Work started on Asam's church in 1733 and was completed in 1746. Four houses were purchased by the brothers and two were demolished to make way for the church. The two others they kept, one to live in and one for the church priest, both of these have a rococo facade.

Since their church was not built to order but as their own private chapel of worship, the brothers were free to incorporate any particular design features they liked.

So they situated the church altar in the west whereas traditionally it is placed in the east. They hung the crucifix lower than usual over the pulpit and constructed just 12 pews.

Despite its small size and private intent, Asam's was still deemed a church, so eventually the brothers were forced to open it to the public. Today visitors can enjoy this fine example of late German Baroque architecture whether they are religious or not. You'll need just half an hour since the church is tiny but mighty.

Highlights include the statue of 14th century Bohemian monk St. Nepomuk stationed above the doorway, he is also depicted in the magnificent ceiling fresco 'Life of Saint Nepomuk' painted by by Cosmas Asam. The high altar is a work of art with spiralling columns, a glass shrine and two angels flanking either side.

The interior is sectioned vertically into three spaces representing humanity, the emperor and God. The design reflects these themes with allegorical statues and scenes moving from darkness to light.

© Flickr / Anne-Lise Heinrichs

Exterior of the Church

Like the ceiling the frescoed walls of the chapel are the work of Cosmas Asam, and the interior has been restored to its original glory since World War II when a bomb attack damaged the church.

#16 Frauenkirche

© Flickr / Thomas Jaehnel

This landmark Catholic Church near the Marienplatz is a much admired icon of Munich. The Frauenkirche, or Church of Our Lady, is easily spotted on the horizon as it is the city's tallest church, with no other buildings permitted to be higher than its two 99 metre towers. Reasons for visiting the church include its beautiful stained-glass windows, Sunday Mass and panoramic views from the south tower of Munich and the Alps.

The Gothic style Frauenkirche is constructed from red brick and took 20 years to build, construction starting in 1468. As Catholic churches go it is unusual for its lack of decoration and, some say, austere interior but it makes up for it in terms of size with a capacity for 20,000 people.

From the outset the project was beset with financial difficulty which is why brick was chosen for the building material as it was cheaper. Pope Sixtus IV had to dip into his pockets in 1479 to allow work on the church to continue.

The church was completed in 1488 but the two towers remained unfinished until 1525 due to a further lack of funds. The Byzantine style domes erected on top of each tower were a cheap fix to stop the rainwater seeping through the ceilings.

But these characteristic domes, instead of the typical Gothic spires of other churches of the period, have given it a unique place in the Munich skyline. They also allowed allied bombers during World War II to pinpoint the city, with one of the towers being severely damaged as a result of bombing.

The church also suffered a collapsed roof. But thanks to major restoration efforts after the war, the church was fully restored in 1994.

Some of the Frauenkirche's unique features include, ten bells in each tower from four different centuries, one of these, the 'Salveglocke' is one of the largest and heaviest bells in Bavaria. Artwork in the church dates between the 14th and 18th centuries, and features paintings and sculptures by Erasmus Grasser, Ignaz Gunther and Jan Polack.

© Wikimedia / Snowwolf55

Interior of the Church

A popular visitor attraction is the Devil's Footstep, a black footprint framed on the marble floor near the entrance. One of the legends (there are a few) says that the devil made a bargain with the builder of the church that he would pay for it on the proviso that it contained no windows.

The builder tricked the devil by positioning the columns so the devil couldn't see the windows from where he stood. The devil was so furious he stamped his foot and left the mark seen today, which you can photograph yourself standing in.

#17 New Town Hall

Photo by DAVID ILIFF. License: CC-BY-SA 3.0

The home of Munich's administration offices since 1874, the New Town Hall (Neues Rathaus) in Marienplatz is also one of the city's most identifiable landmarks. With its imposing cathedral-like tower and Gothic architecture, it dominates the square.

The New Town Hall was commissioned by King Ludwig I who loved neoclassical buildings and patronised many of the Gothic inspired buildings in the city. The Old Town Hall (also in Marienplatz) was deemed simply too small to house all the city officials and construction work started on the New Town Hall in 1867. Twenty-four buildings were demolished in Marienplatz to make way for the massive new building.

Covering over 9,000 square metres and with 400 rooms, the ambitious project was taken in hand by

German-Austrian architect Georg Hauberrisser. Hauberrisser utilised the main facade to showcase the Wittelsbach dynasty with statues inset along its 100 metre length.

Further Gothic detailing includes spires, gargoyles and even a dragon. You can find other examples of Hauberrisser's work in Munich, he also designed the equally ornate St.Pauls Church in Munich's Ludwigskirche district in 1892.

The New Town Hall is not entirely symmetrical because it had extensions added at later dates. The eastern section is made from brick, and the western half is made from limestone, this includes the 85 metre tower which has a viewing platform and the Rathaus-Glockenspiel, a popular tourist attraction, halfway up.

The Glockenspiel is a musical apparatus which performs daily at 11am, 12 noon and 5pm (the latest time is only in summer). The 'stage' is split into two halves and there are two performances consisting of 32 life-sized figures who dance and joust to the tune of 43 bells.

The first show depicts the wedding of Duke William V and Renata of Lorraine in 1568, and the second show is the Schäfflertanz, a plague dance. The entire performance lasts for around 15 minutes after which a small golden rooster comes out and chirps three times to mark the end of the show.

© Flickr / Allen Brewer

The Glockenspiel

You can dine at the New Town Hall at the restaurant 'Ratskeller' on the ground floor which serves traditional Bavarian food with indoor and outdoor courtyard seating, and there is an official tourist information office also on the ground floor. Free city walking tours start outside the New Town Hall daily at 11am.

#18 Hellabrunn Zoo

© Wikimedia / Rufus46

Hellabrunn Zoo is situated in the south of Munich on the river Isar. It has been rated one of the best zoos in Europe for the fact that a good number of enclosures don't rely on cages to contain the animals but moat features instead.

Covering 36 hectares, this zoo is popular with visitors of all ages and can be visited in any season, though summer is the best time for seeing the most variety of animals.

Housing over 750 species and nearly 20,000 animals, one of the zoo's strengths is its biological diversity.

Founded by the Society of the Zoological Garden of Munich, Hellabrunn Zoo was opened in 1911 and designed by Emanuel von Seidl, a landscape architect best known for his mansions and country houses.

The Byzantine style elephant house was one of the original buildings and completed in 1914. This was able to be heated so as to keep the elephants and other animals warm in winter. The zoo closed for a period of time after World War I but reopened again in 1928 under different management.

Heinz Heck, the new director, was a biologist and started a controversial breeding programme to bring back extinct animals using the genes of existing species. With his brother Lutz he created the Heck horse (modeled on an extinct wild horse, the Tarpan) and Heck cattle (modeled on Aurochs, extinct oversized wild cattle).

His most significant achievement though was greatly increasing the numbers of European bison whose numbers were decimated during the war.

Today Heck's breeding work is continued by the zoo which is dedicated to the conservation and breeding of rare species, such as the endangered drill (a short tailed monkey) and silvery gibbon monkeys. A number of other species have also been bred in the zoo including arctic foxes, gorillas, giraffes and elephants.

© Diego Delso, Wikimedia Commons, License CC-BY-SA 3.0

Asian Elephant at Hellabrunn Zoo

Hellabrunn is classed as a Geo-zoo and was the first in the world to organise animals by geography rather than species. It was Heck's vision to create the animals' natural environment as much as possible.

Today visitors are able to meet and greet animals, feed them and attend shows. Popular attractions include the jungle house with chimps and gorillas, the savannah house with giraffes, Dracula's villa (flying bats), and the Polarium with polar bears.

#19 Neue Pinakothek

© Wikimedia / High Contrast

This art museum is well worth a visit, especially on Sundays when the entry fee is just €1. The Neue Pinakothek is one of the musuems in the Kunstareal or 'art area' of Munich which also includes the Alte Pinakothek and Pinakothek der Moderne.

Sandwiched between the classic and modern art spectrums, the Neue Pinakothek focuses on 18th, 19th and early 20th century European art.

The original building was founded by art lover King Ludwig I in 1853, but unlike many of Munich's historical buildings that were able to reconstructed, the museum unfortunately was too damaged to save and its wreckage was removed in 1949.

A replacement museum was eventually built on the site and

opened in 1981. This is a sleek postmodern building made of concrete with a stone facade. It features some design elements taken from the original building, such as arched window detailing.

Architect Alexander von Branca, also included a manmade lake, large plate glass windows, cornerstones and light filled stairwells. The Neue Pinakothek's successful transition has paved the way for other post-war museums.

Today the museum is run by the Bavarian State Painting Collections which has over 3000 European paintings ranging from classicism to art nouveau in its collection.

Around 400 of these paintings and 50 sculptures are showcased at the Neue Pinakothek, especially 19th century and early 20th century works.

Highlights are paintings by the French Impressionists and German Romantics with the big name crowd pleasers like Manet, Picasso, Monet and Van Gogh on display.

But there are plenty of other artists to discover as well, such as Francisco de Goya, Anton Graff and Don José Queraltó.

© Flickr / Rob124

Inside the Neue Pinakothek

This is a well organised museum and art works are efficiently arranged so you shouldn't find yourself wandering aimlessly. A map is available as is an audio guide in multiple languages.

The onsite restaurant Hunsinger is open daily for light meals and coffee. You can also head to the museum's Cedon Bookshop to purchase postcards, gifts and museum memorabilia.

#20 Theatine Church

© Wikimedia / Fczarnowski

If you have time then definitely make the effort to visit the Theatine Church in Odeonsplatz, just opposite the Munich Residenz. This distinctive Roman Catholic church is a well known city symbol and easily recognisable by its yellow Baroque facade.

Even more ornate Baroque splendour awaits the unsuspecting visitor inside with an all-white interior with cupids and ornate plasterwork.

The church was built as a dedication to the birth of Prince Maximilian Emanuel by his parents Ferdinand Maria and Henriette Adelaide of Savoy. The birthday present took a while to eventuate though with construction work taking 27 years from 1663 to 1690.

Built in Italian high-Baroque style, Italian architect Agostino Barelli was inspired by the Sant'Andrea della Valle in Rome.

Even though they were not part of the original plans, two 66 metre high towers were added by his successor Enrico Zuccalli, who also completed a 71 metre high dome to give it extra pizazz.

If that wasn't enough to satisfy, a Flemish father and son team both named François de Cuvilliés, worked on the final finishing touches - a Rococo style facade added in 1765.

François de Cuvilliés the elder also worked on the Residenz Palace and was largely responsible for bringing the graceful Rococo style to Germany.

White stucco decorations abound in the church's interior by Nicolo Petri, alongside white statuary by Wolfgang Leutner, a German sculptor. Paintings are also numerous with examples by important European 17th and 18th century artists Joachim Sandrart, Carlo Cignani and Caspar de Crayer.

Southern German sculptor Andreas Faistenberger created the stark black pulpit and the main altar is decked out in gold with large statues of the Apostles Mark, John, Luke and Matthew.

© Wikimedia / Harro52

Interior of the Church

The Theatine Church houses a number of tombs of the Wittelsbach family including Maximilian I, for whom the church was built, and his parents (they are in the crypt) as well as King Maximilian II and his wife, Queen Marie, who are in a small chapel.

Charles VII the Holy Roman Emperor is also buried here as well as King Otto of Greece, King Ludwig I's second son who was exiled to Bavaria in 1867

Map of Attractions in Central Munich

#1 Marienplatz

#2 Oktoberfest

#4 Deutsches Museum

#7 Munich Residenz

#10 Alte Pinakothek

#11 Hofbrauhaus Munchen

#12 St. Peter's Church

#14 Viktualienmarkt

#15 Asam's Church

#16 Frauenkirche

#17 New Town Hall

#19 Neue Pinakothek

#20 Theatine Church

Map of Attractions in Outer Munich

#3 English Garden

#5 BMW Museum

#6 Nymphenburg Palace

#8 BMW Welt

#9 Allianz Arena

#13 Olympiapark

#18 Hellabrunn Zoo

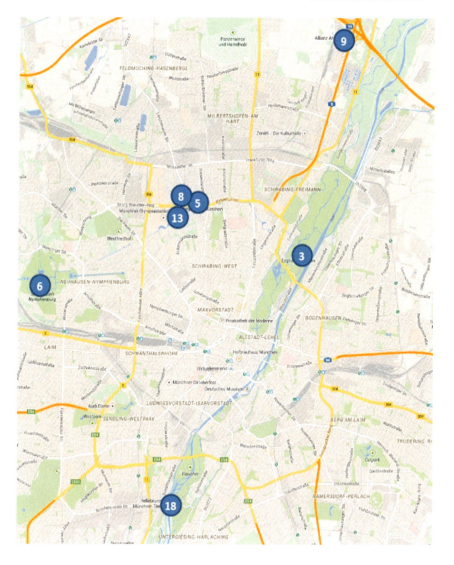

A Note to the Reader

Dear Reader

Thank you for your purchase of this Atsons Travel guide, we hope you have enjoyed reading it!

Please feel free to post an informative, unbiased review on Amazon so that others may benefit from your experience. A Review would be greatly appreciated as it helps us spread the word of our books and attract more fantastic customers such as yourselves.

Also your feedback is invaluable to us, as we work hard to serve you and continually improve our customers' experience.

Sincerely

Atsons Travel Guides

Made in the USA
Middletown, DE
10 April 2018